CANADIAN

Writers in Action

HANDBOOK

Evelyn Steinberg

Senior Consultant:
Brenda Newcombe

gagelearning

National Library of Canada Cataloguing in Publication

Main entry under title:

Steinberg, Evelyn, 1944-
    Writers in action handbook / Evelyn Steinberg

Includes index.
ISBN 0-7715-1756-4
ISBN 0-7715-1755-6 N.S.

    1. English language—Composition and exercises—Juvenile literature. I. Title.

LB1576.S73 2002   808.042
C2002-901775-0

Acknowledgements

Every reasonable effort has been made to trace ownership of copyrighted material. Information that would enable the publisher to correct any reference in future editions would be appreciated.

23 "Water Spirit" from *Cloudwalker: Contemporary Native American Stories* by Joel Monture. © 1996 by Joel Monture. Fulcrum Publishing, Inc., Golden, CO. All rights reserved. **25** "Atlantic Seashore," excerpt from *At the Seashore* by Pamela Hickman. © 1996 by Pamela Hickman. **27** Excerpt from *Northern Lights: The Soccer Trails.* © 1993 Michael Arvaarluk Kusugak. Published by Annick Press Ltd. Reprinted with permission of Annick Press Ltd. **30** Excerpt from *The Wreck of the Dispatch* by Janet Lunn. Reprinted with permission of the author and Lee Davis Creal, Literary Agent. **37** Excerpt from *Balloon Science* by Etta Kaner. © 1989. **39** "I Eat Kids Yum Yum," from *Garbage Delight* (MacMillan of Canada, 1977). Copyright © 1977 Dennis Lee. With permission of the author. **39** "A Use for a Moose," from *Falling Up* by Shel Silverstein. **40** "This Canada" from *Save the World For Me* by Maxine Tynes. Reprinted with permission of the author. **41** "That duck, bobbing up" by Joso from *Cricket Songs Japanese Haiku* translated by Henry Behn. © 1992 Prescott Behn, Pamela Behn Adam and Peter Behn. **50** "Sea Otters," by Petrina Mutti. Reprinted with permission of the author. **55** "Australia's Crabby Ants," by kidsnewsroom.org. **120** "The Red-Headed League" from *Mysteries of Sherlock Holmes* by Sir Arthur Conan Doyle, adapted by Judith Conaway. © 1982 by Random House, Inc.

We acknowledge the financial support of the Government of Canada through the Book Publishing Industry Development Program for our publishing activities.

We acknowledge the Government of Ontario through the Ontario Media Development Corporation's Ontario Book Initiative.

Project Team:
Joe Banel, David Friend, Nicole Woodrow

Cover and page design:
Pages Design Ltd.

Illustrations:
Stephen MacEachern

ISBN 0-7715-**1756-4**
ISBN 0-7715-**1755-6** N.S.

2 3 4 5 FP 06 05 04 03

Written, Printed, and Bound in Canada

Table of Contents

Part 1 — How Writers Write:
The Writing Process

Part 2 — What Writers Write:
Forms

Part 3 — How Writers Research

Part 4 — How Writers Improve Their Style

Part 5　How Writers Edit Their Work

Word Use and Spelling

Grammar

To the Student

We just want to tell you a bit about this book. It's the kind of book that can help you with your writing. It's not the kind of book that you read from cover to cover.

Have you ever had trouble getting started with your writing? Do you sometimes find it hard to organize your thoughts? Are you unsure of how to edit? Then use the index and table of contents to help you locate what you need.

Most authors write their thoughts in several ways before they are satisfied. You will need to do that too. Writing takes a lot of time, patience, and practice, but there is always a feeling of pride when you do your best work!

Happy writing!

Part 1

How Writers Write:
The Writing Process

Contents

Developing Ideas

One of the first tasks you will face when you write something is deciding what you want to say. This is true even when someone else suggests an idea or topic for your writing. Here are a few ways of developing ideas:

→ Think about your own experiences and interests.
→ Brainstorm ideas with classmates.
→ Skim books or, with supervision, surf the Web.
→ Review ideas in your writing folder, journal, or writer's notebook.
→ Talk with friends, family members, or your teacher.
→ Think about books, movies, TV programs, or songs you know.
→ Create a thought web or other drawing.

Strategy

How to Brainstorm

Brainstorming is a strategy that helps you develop a lot of ideas very quickly. Brainstorming works best in a small group.

1. Jot down every idea that you can think of, even if the idea seems silly.

2. Add it to the ideas of others.

3. Do not judge or criticize ideas.

Planning Your Writing

When you are working on a longer piece of writing, it can be helpful to make a plan before you start. A simple plan could include

→ a few notes listing your ideas
→ a list of some sources of information you want to check
→ a list of the facts you want to present

In other cases, you might make a more detailed plan. For example, if you are working on a long report, you might start by creating an outline. An outline shows how your writing will be organized.

Sample Outline

Title: Snakes That Bite

Introduction: Some snakes are poisonous.

1st paragraph: Why snakes have venom

2nd paragraph: Five poisonous snakes

3rd paragraph: Understanding snakes

Conclusion: Poisonous snakes are important.

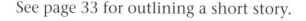

See page 33 for outlining a short story.

Drafting

The drafting stage is the stage when you start to express your ideas. Feel free to experiment and make changes as you write your draft.

→ Don't worry about getting everything right. The most important thing is to get your ideas flowing. You can always make changes later.

→ If you are writing your draft by hand, use only one side of the paper and skip lines. This will give you room to write your changes.

→ You should look at your plan or outline as you write, but you don't have to follow it exactly. Writers often get new ideas while they draft.

Strategy

How to Solve Writer's Block

If you don't know what to write or how to get started, you might have writer's block. Here are ways you can solve the problem:

1. Leave the part you are stuck on and work on a different part. If you need to, start in the middle or at the end.

2. Sit down for a few minutes and write whatever comes into your head about your topic. Don't stop, even if you repeat yourself.

3. Discuss your ideas with a classmate. He or she might have a comment or question that will spark new ideas.

Revising

Did you know that some writers rework a piece of writing many times? This process is called revising. At this stage, you take a step back and look at your writing once again. You can think about how you might improve your work by making changes.

You can revise your writing on your own or with a partner.

Here are some suggestions.

1. Read Aloud

Slowly read your writing out loud to yourself. Does it sound right for your purpose and audience?

2. Ask Questions

Check your writing by asking questions:

→ Does my writing make sense?
→ Does my opening (called the lead) grab the reader's attention?
→ Are my ideas in the best order?
→ Could I find better words to express my ideas?
→ Did I leave out anything important?
→ Did I repeat information?
→ Does my ending wrap up my ideas?

3. Read Again

Read your writing out loud again. You might try this with a friend. Listen for

→ words or sentences that sound wrong
→ repeated phrases
→ words that don't add anything important

4. Make the Revisions

If you wrote your draft using a computer, then making your revisions is fairly simple because it's easy to add, cut, and move text around. But you still may want to print your draft. You can then make changes on paper before making them on screen. If your work is handwritten, you can make the revisions right on the page.

Here is an example of how you revise your work.

> *Need a stronger lead.*
> *Tell what she looks like?*
>
> Donna is a nice person. We used to play tag every
>
> day after school. I met her when I was in grade two.
> *move up*
>
> But I do not like her sister.

Writer's Tip

Leave Some Time

Try to leave some time between revising and editing. If you put your writing aside for a day, or even a few hours, you will have "fresh eyes" to spot any problems.

Editing

The purpose of editing is to make sure that each sentence makes sense. It is an important part of polishing your writing so that it is ready for people to read. This is the stage when you focus on sentence structure, language, and grammar.

The sample below shows the changes you make while editing.

There͛s nobody like a best friend, a best friend cheer͛
you up when you feel bad. My best ~~buds~~ friends are Adrian,

Spencer, Sanjiv, and Tess.

When you edit, it is best to reread your writing more than once. Focus on something different each time. Here are the things you focus on while editing.

Sentences	• See Sentences, p. 109; Sentence Fragments, p. 112; Run-on Sentences, p. 113.
Language	• See Formal and Informal Language, p. 77; Figurative Language, p. 80; Inclusive Language, p. 97.
Grammar	• See Grammar, p. 99.

Proofreading

Proofreading involves looking at each word and punctuation mark and fixing spelling, capitalization, and punctuation errors. You should also think about whether or not you have used words properly.

See Commonly Confused Words, page 91; Spelling/Word Study, page 94; Punctuation, page 117; Capitalization, page 126.

The key to being a good proofreader is to read slowly. Here are some other suggestions:

→ If you wrote using a computer, print a copy and write any changes on the pages. Don't proofread on screen.

→ Use a ruler and slide it down the page line by line.

→ Read your work backwards from the last sentence to the first.

→ Draw a circle around any words that don't look right and use a dictionary to check the spelling.

→ Read the work aloud to listen for proper punctuation.

→ Use a proofreading checklist.

Writer's Tip

Use a Computer

Computers have tools to help with editing and proofreading. Spell checkers, thesauruses, and grammar checkers can help you find errors and correct them.

Publishing

After you make the final corrections to your writing, it's time to publish! Publishing involves making a good copy of your work that is ready for people to read.

There are many ways of publishing your work. You might display it on a bulletin board, submit it to a contest, add it to the library, include it in a class anthology, or post it on the school's Web site.

When you are ready to publish, ask yourself how you can make your work interesting to look at and easy to read. Here are a few ideas:

→ Design a colourful cover that attracts attention.
→ Add a table of contents to tell readers where to find things.
→ Insert headings and bulleted lists to highlight information.
→ Include graphs, illustrations, and diagrams that can help readers understand what you mean. Be sure to include labels and captions.

You can see what these ideas look like on the next page.

If you finish your writing by hand, use neat printing or cursive writing. Always use printing for labels and captions. If you use a computer, experiment with different fonts for titles, headings, and text. **Bold type**, <u>underlining</u>, and colour are effective ways of drawing the reader's attention.

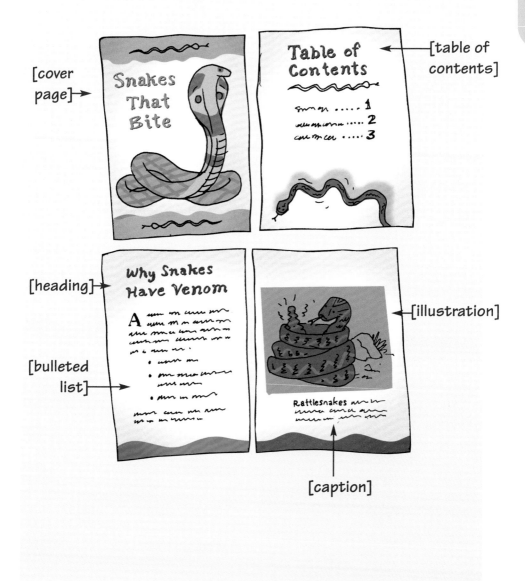

[cover page] → Snakes That Bite

[table of contents] → Table of Contents
.... 1
.... 2
.... 3

[heading] → Why Snakes Have Venom

[bulleted list]

[illustration]

Rattlesnakes

[caption]

Part 2

What Writers Write: Forms

Contents

Types of Writing

There are four main types of writing—narrative writing, expository writing, descriptive writing, and persuasive writing.

TYPES OF WRITING

Narrative
- to tell a story

Descriptive
- to create a clear picture

Expository
- to give information

Persuasive
- to convince the reader

Narrative Writing

The purpose of narrative writing is to tell a story. Novels and short stories are examples of narrative writing. Narrative writing is also used in fairy tales, fables, and diary entries.

Narrative writing usually has

→ a beginning, middle, and end
→ one or more characters
→ a problem that needs to be solved

Helpful hints

1. You can write in the first person (**I** went to the park) or third person (**She** went to the park).

2. Describe the setting clearly so the reader can imagine it.

3. Describe the characters' appearance and personality.

4. Include dialogue to create interest.

See Short Story, page 30.

Louis DesChamp suddenly rolled off the log he was sitting on. He was laughing so hard his stomach began to ache, and tears rolled down his brown cheeks. His father, Rene, had just put the old wood and canvas canoe in the lake by the short dock. When Rene stepped in, the bottom broke, and he fell right through the canoe. He stood up to his waist in water, holding a paddle, with a surprised look on his face.

It was springtime in Maniwaki, Québec, a land of forests, lakes, and rivers, which had been home to the Cree people for countless generations. It was also home to the majestic moose, loon, beaver, raven, and eagle. The rivers and lakes were full of trout, salmon, and bass, and it was a great thrill to go fishing after the spring thaws melted the ice on the lakes. Today, Louis was eager to go fishing, but seeing his father fall through the canoe was so funny.

"Hey, Dad," he called, regaining his voice, "catch any fish yet?"

Rene smiled and placed the paddle on the dock. "Help me get out of here."

From "Water Spirit"
by Joel Monture

Expository Writing

The purpose of expository writing is to give information. When you write a history report for school, you are using expository writing. Instructions, explanations, and newspaper articles are other forms of expository writing.

Expository writing usually has

→ an introduction, body, and conclusion
→ a main idea (**thesis**)
→ information that develops the main idea, such as facts, quotations, and statistics

Helpful hints

1. Arrange ideas in an order that makes sense, for example, most important to least important.

2. Give each paragraph a main idea and details about the idea.

3. Focus on facts, not opinions.

4. Do not use personal references.

Incorrect	**My** report is about sea otters.
Correct	**This** report is about sea otters.

See Report, page 48.

An outing to the seashore is a great way to have fun and meet some of nature's most fascinating creatures. Whether you dig in the mud, poke into rock pools, paddle in the shallows, or just lie on the beach, many new adventures await you at the shore.

There are two tides per day on the Atlantic shore. It is a bit longer than six hours between high tide and low tide. Certain shorelines, particularly along the Bay of Fundy and Minas Basin, have extremely high tides that come in very quickly. The best time to explore the shorelines below the cliffs in these areas is after high tide, when the tide is going out.

From "Atlantic Seashore" by Pamela Hickman

Forms

Descriptive Writing

Descriptive writing uses words to create a clear picture of something in the reader's mind. It is used to describe people, places, things, and events. A character profile is one kind of descriptive writing. Descriptive writing is often used in novels, stories, and poems.

Descriptive writing usually has

→ strong words that give specific details (The **rusty old** mountain bike **clanked** to a stop.)

→ words that appeal to the different senses (sight, sound, smell, taste, and touch)

→ an organized way of describing (most important to least important)

Helpful hints

1. Think about how you want the reader to feel while reading the description.

2. List all the details you can think of, and then choose the ones that are most important.

3. Use strong verbs, adverbs, and adjectives that will help you catch the reader's interest.

4. Try using similes, metaphors, and personification.

See Figurative Language, page 80.

In the fall, ice forms on the lakes and the sea. At night, when the sky is clear, you can see the stars, millions of them, twinkling through the moonlight. And sometimes you can see the droppings of the stars come streaking across the sky and disappear before they reach the horizon.

Sometimes the northern lights came out. They are thin strands of light, thousands of thin strands of light, that move about from here to there like thousands of people running around, following one another.

From "Northern Lights: The Soccer Trails"
by Michael Arvaarluk Kusugak

Forms

Persuasive Writing

The purpose of persuasive writing is to convince the reader to agree with your point of view. It is used in some reports and is also found in movie reviews and in many speeches.

Persuasive writing usually has

→ an introduction, body, and conclusion
→ a main idea (**thesis**)
→ strong arguments that prove the main idea (facts and reasons)

Helpful hints

1. State your point of view clearly at the start.

2. Include at least three good arguments.

3. Choose a tone that works well (for example, serious, humorous, angry, or excited).

4. Summarize your point of view with a strong statement.

Sample Persuasive Piece

Did you know that fifty per cent of the Earth's species will have vanished in the next 100 years? Animals that seem very common to us like eagles and wolves are disappearing from our planet because we are slowly killing them. In time, their disappearance will be harmful to our planet.

Our planet is like a bicycle. If you were to take away a part of it, like the chain or wheels, it wouldn't work well. In the same way, if one animal becomes extinct it affects our whole ecosystem. All animals contribute to our environment. Even spiders do! They spin webs that catch insects.

Many years ago there was a bird called the dodo. This bird was found on an island in the Indian Ocean. The people who found these strange looking birds hunted and killed them. They also brought different animals like dogs and pigs into the dodo's habitat. Today there are no more dodos to be found. Other animals that are extinct are the Tasmanian tiger and the great auk (a type of flightless bird like a penguin that was once found in Canada).

Animals that are endangered or threatened (which means they might become extinct) include the grizzly bear, panda, gorilla, tiger, and humpback whale. Can you imagine a world without pandas or whales?

If we want to make sure that the animals we have on our planet today do not all die, we have to stop hunting them and clean up our environment. We must also make sure that we do not take away their homes by building our houses on the land that they use. We need animals to help the planet run well.

Short Story

A short story is a fictional tale that offers a snapshot of life. It often focusses on a conflict.

Here are some suggestions to follow if you are writing a short story.

1. Write a Strong Lead

The beginning of your story—called your lead—should catch the reader's attention. It often gives the setting, characters, and the main conflict. Here are some story starters:

→ an exciting event — Lightning flashed and the rain poured down from the sky.

→ a description — The dewy grass sparkled under the warm spring sun.

Here is an example of a story with a strong lead:

> "Annie, Annie," cried John, "there must be a shipwreck! I can see a whole long mast heading toward the rocks. Come quick!"
>
> Gathering up her long skirt, Annie came running toward the shore.
>
> "Oh, John, to be sure it's a wreck and small wonder in such a storm. Can there be a single body left alive, do you think? Quick, go fetch Pa while I get the boat in the water."
>
> From *The Wreck of the Dispatch* by Janet Lunn

2. Use Description

Clear descriptions make a story come alive. Use words that help the reader see, hear, smell, taste, and feel what you are describing:

Alicia cradled the fragile bird in her cupped hands.

The alarm clock screeched like a thousand rusty gates.

A gust of wind carried the salty smell of the ocean.

3. Introduce Conflict

Most stories have a conflict—a problem that has to be solved. Here are some examples of conflict:

A hero tries to outsmart a villain.

A character has to face his fear of the dark.

Two people have to work together to fight a flood.

4. Include Dialogue

The words characters speak to each other are called dialogue. It shows what the characters are like and how they feel about each other.

"I won't finish this in time," groaned Mary.

"Don't worry," said Kim. "I'm happy to help you."

See Quotation Marks, page 120.

5. End by Solving the Conflict

Most stories end by showing how the conflict turns out. This helps the reader feel that the story is truly over. Here are some examples:

The hero captures the villain.

A character finds his way home through a dark forest.

Two people save their farm from a flood.

6. Choose an Effective Title

An effective title gets the reader's attention and gives a clue about the story. To get a fresh idea of what your story is about, look back on what you have written. Brainstorm as many titles as you can. Choose the best one from your list. Look at the examples below.

Lost in the Woods

Mountain of Doom

Cliffhanger

Strategy

How to Outline a Story

A story map can help you plan your story. To create a map, you have to think about the main parts of your story before you start. See the sample story map on the next page.

Sample Story Map

Title: Cheater on Wheels
Author: Joseph V.

Setting

Place: my town
Time: the present

Characters

Cynthia: 12 years old, clever, athletic, the main character
Ken: Cynthia's nasty neighbour, 11 years old
Kala: Cynthia's best friend, 12 years old, good at repairing bikes
Martin: Cynthia's brother, 8 years old, a pest, but can be helpful

Story Conflict

Ken plans to cheat in a local bike race. He doesn't want Cynthia to win again.

The Beginning

Ken brags to Cynthia and Kala that he will win the next bike race.

The Middle: Main Plot Events

- Kala overhears Ken planning to cheat.
- Kala and Cynthia figure out how to stop Ken.
- Martin almost gives away the plan.
- The judges catch Ken cheating during the race.

The Ending

Cynthia wins the race.

Character Profile

> **A character profile is a short description of a person's abilities, character, or career. This person may be a real person or a fictional character.**

A good character profile will help readers feel as if they have met the person you are describing. Here are some suggestions to help you write a character profile.

→ Keep the opening short and simple with lots information.

→ Describe the place where the person lives or works.

→ Try to bring the person to life. Describe his or her qualities and give examples.

→ Use quotations—something the person or character actually says. See Quotation Marks, page 120.

→ Include details that tell what kind of person he or she is, for example, his or her likes and dislikes.

→ Sum up your impression of the person.

When Gary Pearson looks up from his drawing table, he has a big grin on his face. Gary is an animator who works for the CBC (Canadian Broadcasting Corporation). His office walls are covered with the humorous cartoons he creates. Since childhood, Gary has been interested in cartoons and animated films. "I watched a lot of cartoons on television. I liked to draw the characters. I would draw, draw, and draw all the time," he says. To become an animator, Gary studied graphic arts and illustration at Sheridan College in Toronto for three years. His animation has been used in *Sesame Park*, *Mr. Dressup*, *Hockey Night in Canada*, and many other TV shows and films. You can tell by Gary's grin that he loves his work. "Sitting at a table and drawing cartoon characters—that's a pretty good job!"

Forms

Instructions

Instructions explain how to do something. The audience is usually someone who has never done it before.

Follow these steps to create clear, easy-to-follow instructions:

1. Explain the purpose.

2. List all the materials needed.

3. Describe exactly how the activity is done. List each step in order.

4. Make the directions clear and simple. Start each instruction with an action verb.
   Glue the paper onto the wood.

5. Include illustrations if that will help the reader understand what to do. Label any illustrations clearly.

6. If there are any dangers, tell the reader how to avoid them.
   Do not touch the powder. It is poisonous.

Cold Air Experiment

Which takes up less space, warm air or cold air? Make a prediction, then try this balloon experiment at home.

You'll need
- a balloon
- a felt pen
- a measuring tape
- a refrigerator

1. Inflate the balloon and tie it tightly.
2. Measure the balloon around its widest part. Mark the balloon with a felt pen where you measured it.
3. Put the balloon in the freezer overnight.
4. In the morning, measure the chilled balloon around its widest part.

From *Balloon Science*
by Etta Kaner

Forms

Poetry

Poetry uses carefully chosen words and phrases to express ideas, images, and feelings. The words are usually arranged in short lines to produce a pattern or special look. You can write a poem to tell a story, share a feeling, describe something, or just have fun with words.

There are many different forms of poetry. Poetry offers you the opportunity to experiment.

→ Some poems rhyme, but many have no rhyme at all.
→ Some poems have a regular beat. Others don't.
→ Some poems look neat and tidy, and some look wild.

When you write a poem, here are some things you can try.

1. Experiment with Imagery

You can "paint" pictures or images in the reader's mind in many different ways. Strong nouns, adjectives, adverbs, and verbs can be very effective.

Water gushing from a
　　　yellow hydrant
A flood rushing
　　　down the sidewalk ...
Washes away summer heat.

2. Experiment with Rhyme

When two words have a similar sound, they rhyme, like **bold** and **cold.** In a rhyming poem, the rhymes usually go at the end of the lines. The rhyming can follow different patterns. AABB and ABAB are two common rhyme patterns.

A child went out one **day**	A
She only went to **play**	A
A mighty monster came **along**	B
And sang its mighty monster **song**.	B

Dennis Lee

3. Experiment with Rhythm

Some poems have a strong beat that you can hear when you read them out loud. This beat is the poem's rhythm. In the poem below, the words and syllables that get a heavier beat are underlined. Read it aloud to hear its rhythm.

The antlers of a standing moose,

As everybody knows,

Are just the perfect place to hang

Your wet and drippy clothes.

It's quick and cheap, but I must say

I've lost a lot of clothes that way.

Shel Silverstein

4. Experiment with Free Verse

Free verse poems do not have a regular rhyme or rhythm. Free verse poems often sound like someone talking.

Look at the poem on the next page for an example of a free verse poem.

Tell me what this country is
this Canada
this nation of same and different
    of faces and voices and places
     and trees
    of east and west
    of Inuit, Aboriginal
    of French and English
    and everyone else in between.

Tell me what this country feels
this Canada
this nation of together and separate
    of push and pull
    of *bonjour* and good morning
    of stars and stripes beckoning
    of northern lights showing tears
    of the first people.

Show me a map of this country
this Canada
charted with a past that beckons
    and keeps us
charted with rivers of hopes
    and dreams
shaped by winds of change
shaded with the faces of you and of us
as we move toward new freedoms
as we come into our own
This Canada.

"This Canada" from *Save the World for Me* by Maxine Tynes

5. Experiment with Language

Here are a few ways of having fun with language:

→ **Similes** make interesting comparisons using *like* or *as*.

The wind howled **like** a pack of wolves.
See Simile, page 80.

→ **Onomatopoeia** uses words that imitate sounds.

thud, chirp, bang
See Onomatopoeia, page 81.

→ **Alliteration** puts words together that start with the same sound.

Fat **f**lakes of snow **f**loated to the ground.
See Alliteration, page 81.

Strategy

How to Write Haiku

The haiku is a form of poetry that has been written in Japan for centuries. Haiku freeze one moment in time, like a snapshot. Haiku are often about nature and the seasons.

Haiku consist of three short lines and 17 syllables (5 + 7 + 5).

That duck, bobbing up	**5 syllables**
from the green deeps of a pond,	**7 syllables**
has seen something strange.	**5 syllables**

Joso

Letters

A letter is a written or printed message that is usually put into an envelope and delivered by mail.

There are two kinds of letters: the **friendly letter** and the **business letter**. Here is some information about each kind.

Friendly Letter

Purpose	• to keep in touch • to share information and good wishes • to say thank you
Audience	• people you know well • friends and family members
How to Organize the Letter	• use different paragraphs for each idea
Tone	• use a personal tone, as if you are having a conversation with the person • use slang expressions if you want

426 Elm Lane
Halifax NS B3H 4P6
October 12, 20--

←[sender's address]
←[date]

Dear Gran,

←[greeting]

    I love my new sweater that you sent for my birthday. I have already worn it three times because I love it so much. You really are an excellent knitter.

    Yesterday my friend Sharma and I went to a movie. It was all animation and it made us laugh so much. Do you remember Sharma? You met her when you visited us last summer.

    Next week my class is going on an overnight camping trip. I hope the weather stays warm!!! Thank you again for my sweater.

Love,

←[closing]

Jeannie

←[signature]

Jeannie Roumanis
426 Elm Lane
Halifax NS B3H 4P6

←[sender's address]

Helen Roumanis
412 Main Street
Vancouver BC V5T 1Z3

←[recipient's address]

Forms

Business Letter

Purpose	• to ask for information • to buy something • to make a complaint • to make a request
Audience	• businesses or organizations • people you don't know
How to Organize the Letter	• start with an introduction that tells the purpose of the letter • give the details of your message • ask for any information you need or state an action that should be taken • be brief • give specific instructions
Tone	• use a polite tone, even if you are making a complaint • use formal language

Devon Wilson   ←[sender]
1216 Glen Road
Hamilton ON L8S 3M9

20-- 01 14   ←[date]

Lisa Cardinal   ←[recipient]
Adventure Publishing Company
123 Calvert Street NW
Calgary AB T2K 2E6

Dear Ms. Cardinal: ←[opening]

I read about a new book that your company has published. It is called *Heroes of Our Land*. I am really interested in it and I would like to buy a copy. I am sending you a money order for $12.47. This includes the tax.

Please send the book to me at my address on this letter.

Thank you very much.

Yours truly,   ←[closing]

Devon Wilson   ←[signature]

Devon Wilson

Devon Wilson   ←[sender]
1216 Glen Road
Hamilton ON L8S 3M9

Lisa Cardinal   ←[recipient]
Adventure Publishing Company
123 Calvert Street NW
Calgary AB T2K 2E6

E-mail

> The word e-mail is short for "electronic mail." An e-mail is a letter written on a computer, that is sent to another person's computer using the Internet.

Writing an e-mail is similar to writing a letter, but an e-mail travels more quickly than a letter. An e-mail can reach its destination in seconds—even when you send it halfway around the world.

Here are some suggestions for writing an e-mail:

→ Let the reader know what the e-mail is about by typing the topic in the subject line.

→ Use short paragraphs to get your message across quickly.

→ Enter all the addresses in the "To" line. You can send your e-mail to more than one person at the same time.

→ E-mail between friends often contains short forms of longer sayings.

BOL	means	best of luck
JK	means	just kidding
TTFN	means	ta ta for now
BTW	means	by the way

From: Janice Smith
To: Joel Rubin; Hailey Stuart
Sent: May 2, 2002
Subject: Our Play

Hi guys,
Let's get together Wednesday after school to rehearse the play. We don't have too much time to get ready. Only a week! Don't forget we still have to do our costumes. Joel, can we meet at your house?

Write back and let me know if you will be there.

TTFN
Jannie

Report

A report tells about a specific topic. Often the writer has to do some research to learn about the topic. Reports can be written or oral.

Writing a report (sometimes called a **project**) is an important way of showing your skills as a learner. Most reports are written in a formal style. For example, you don't use first-person pronouns such as *I*, *we*, or *me*.

To write a report, you usually move through some or all of the stages below.

1. Getting Started

Most reports require a lot of work. That's why it is important to take some time to plan. First, make sure you understand your **topic**. It can also be helpful to create an outline of your report. See the sample outline on page 12.

2. Researching

Once you have a plan for your report, you can start to collect and organize information. When you have finished your research, look at your outline again. You may want to change it to match your information. See The Research Process, page 59.

3. Drafting the Report

A report has three parts:

→ The **introduction** explains what the report is about and what the reader will learn. It may also state an idea or argument.

→ The **body** presents the information you selected. Each paragraph should focus on one main idea. It should provide details to support that idea. Often the body will also include visuals, such as graphs, photos, and diagrams. Remember to place the paragraphs in an order that makes sense. See Organizing Information, page 66.

→ The **conclusion** gives a summary of the main ideas. It usually gives your final thoughts about the topic.

Writer's Tip

Use Transition Words

Transition words are words that help readers follow the flow of your thought. They connect sentence to sentence and paragraph to paragraph.

See Transition Words, page 76.

4. Adding the Extras

→ If your report is long, you may need a table of contents.

→ If you have a lot of information, you can break your report into different sections. Give each section its own heading.

→ Be sure to tell the reader when you have taken ideas from another source. You do this by using quotation marks and by creating a bibliography. See Giving Credit, page 68.

Sea Otters

The sea otter is a member of the weasel family. Some people call the sea otter "the teddy bear of the sea." For centuries, hunters killed sea otters for their soft, thick fur. In 1989, the biggest oil spill in U.S. history killed thousands of sea otters.

Sea otters weigh up to 39 kg and can reach up to 1.5 m in length. Sea otters have very thick fur. They have as many as 18 hairs emerging from a single hair follicle. Sea otters do not have blubber found in all other marine mammals. They have a streamlined appearance. Sea otters have small round heads and a long heavy body. They have a thick tapering tail that is flat on the bottom and their eyes are dark. Their noses are a flat diamond shape. They have little pointed ears which close when they dive.

Sea otters once lived off the Pacific coast as far south as California. The sea otters' habitat is where the water is about 15 to 23 m. The area is a place where the sea otter will be protected from harsh winds and other weather conditions. Islands, rock reefs, and kelp forest are some of the barriers that help calm the water.

Sea otters eat sea urchins, molluscs, crustaceans, and fish. Sea otters break shells of invertebrates with rocks they bring from the ocean floor. The sea otter floats on its back and balances the rock on its chest and pounds the shell on the rock until the shell breaks. Mating occurs in spring and summer and the young are born the following spring. When the sea otter is ready to dive, it takes a deep breath of air and rolls forward into the water and holds its paws across its chest as it moves its body up and down.

Did you know that sea otters are dying in large numbers? We are building our homes, farms, and industry over their habitat. However, if we want to protect the sea otter, we have to make sure that it has a place to live.

An oral report is a report that is spoken to an audience.

An oral report can be a great way to share information. As a speaker, you have direct contact with your audience. You can hold their interest in different ways—with your voice or with arm gestures, for example.

If you feel a bit nervous about speaking to an audience, don't worry. It's normal! You can end your worries by being well prepared. Here are some ideas to help you make a successful oral report:

→ Make jot notes on note cards.
→ Memorize the main points you want to make.
→ Rehearse your presentation so you feel comfortable.
→ Use props or visuals that add to your presentation.
→ Speak clearly, slowly, and loudly.
→ Look at your audience.
→ Try to involve the audience in your presentation.
→ Be prepared to answer questions about your topic.

Newspaper Article

A newspaper article is an information piece that usually tells about a current event or issue.

People read newspaper articles to get news about current events, sports, and entertainment.

1. Start with a Lead

The lead of a newspaper article gives a key detail that makes the reader want to know more. It can be one sentence or a whole paragraph.

2. Answer the Reader's Questions

A good newspaper article presents all the main facts that a reader would want to know about an event. It answers these questions—Who? What? When? Where? Why? and How?

To answer these questions, you may need to interview people who were involved in the event.

3. Put the Most Important Information First

Did you know that many people read only the first part of a newspaper article? That's why writers try to put all the important information at the beginning.

Strategy

How to Use the 5Ws and H

The 5Ws and H can help you plan and write an article.
First, answer these questions.

Who was involved?

What happened?

When did it happen?

Where did it happen?

Why did it happen?

and

How did it happen?

Second, make sure the answers to those questions
are in your article.

4. Create a Headline

A short, snappy headline catches the reader's attention. It
should sum up the main idea of the article.

Canucks on Thin Ice

K9 hero saves the day

Stones still rolling

Australia's Crabby Ants ←[headline]

On Wednesday, April 10, 2002, officials in Australia announced that half of the crab population on Australia's Christmas Island may have been destroyed over the past few years. How? Because the ferocious ants that reside ←[lead] on the island are eating all the crabs. Christmas Island's crabs are famous because every year millions of them swim far into the ocean to spawn. Afterwards, they come back to the island.

The ants on the island, which are killing the crabs, are known as "Crazy Ants." They have very long legs and hearty appetites. About five years ago these ants started growing in numbers, reproducing very quickly. They now have big colonies in about 25% of Christmas Island's rain forest.

It may seem hard to believe that some little ants can kill so many crabs in a few years. But these ants actually spit acid! They use the acid to blind the crabs. Then, while the crabs are confused, the ants quickly devour them.

Nobody knows how many crabs were originally on Christmas Island, but now there are about 40 million. There may have been as many as 80 million crabs at one time. Environmental specialists are worried that the ants will eat all of the crabs.

From Kidsnewsroom

Forms

Response

A response describes the writer's thoughts and feelings about something, such as a book, event, or issue.

In school, you may often be asked to write a response to a story, a poem, an experience, a news event, or an important issue. There are two kinds of response—a personal response and a critical response.

1. Responding Personally

When you respond personally to something, you explain what it makes you think about and how it makes you feel. Ask yourself questions like these:

→ How did I feel as I read this piece?
→ Did this piece remind me of something in my own life?
→ Is this story like other stories I know?
→ Does this piece connect with an issue I know?

Here is an example of a personal response to the book *Charlotte's Web*:

> I liked the part in *Charlotte's Web* when Charlotte tells Wilbur that everything will be all right. It reminded me of when my grandmother had a talk with me before she moved.

2. Responding Critically

Our world is filled with texts such as books, magazines, ads, TV shows, and movies. These texts shape the way people think and act. When you respond critically to a text, you ask questions to help you understand how it affects people.

→ **Who created the text and why?** Answering this question can help you see the biases within a text. For example, you probably wouldn't trust a movie review written by the star's mother!

→ **What does the text say?** A text has more than one message. Imagine that you view a TV ad about a new fruit drink called Slurpy. On the surface, the ad says that Slurpy tastes great. Under the surface, the ad might suggest that drinking Slurpy will make people happy and popular.

→ **How does the text influence the audience?** Every text presents ideas about what the world is like. For example, in an action movie, all the main characters might be men. This presents a false assumption that women aren't heroic.

Writer's Tip

Show the Evidence

Providing evidence will make your response stronger. You can

- **refer directly to the text**
- **use a quotation from the text**
- **draw on your personal knowledge**

Part 3

How Writers Research

Contents

The Research Process

Imagine you have decided to investigate earth science. How will you start?

First, you will have to plan your research. When you research, you are looking for information.

Like writing, researching is a process. That means researching is made up of several different stages. Remember, you won't necessarily work through all the stages every time you research.

The diagram below shows the different stages in the research process.

The Research Process

Narrowing a Topic

Giving Credit

Locating Information

Organizing Information

Recording Information

Narrowing a Topic

When you begin to research, you usually have a general topic in mind. For example, you and your classmates might be investigating earth science. The general topic of earth science is too big to research. Before you start, you have to make your focus more specific. Here are some suggestions that can help you narrow a topic:

→ Look through an encyclopedia, textbook, or browse the Internet. You might get a topic idea from a chapter title, a heading, or an index entry.

→ Make a list of questions about the topic that you want to answer. One of your questions could become the focus of a narrower topic.

→ Use an organizer such as a web or tree and write down what you know about the topic. One of the entries on your tree might give you an idea for a narrower topic.

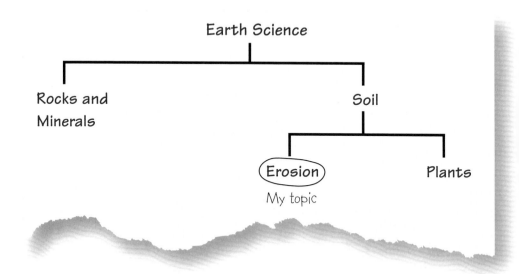

Locating Information

When you are comfortable with your topic, it is time to begin your research. First, you have to find information that suits your needs. Here are the most useful places to look.

The Library

One of the best sources of information is your classroom, school, or community library. The library has a wealth of resources you can check:

encyclopedias	CD-ROMs	books
magazines	newspapers	the Internet
vertical files	films	atlases
videos	audiotapes	brochures

Libraries have an electronic or card catalogue that lists books by title, author, and subject. Subject listings are the most useful. Don't hesitate to ask the librarian for help with your search. Here is a sample title search in an electronic catalogue.

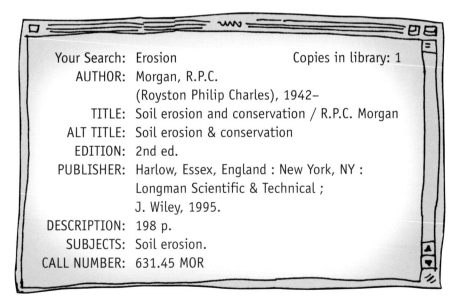

```
Your Search:   Erosion                    Copies in library: 1
   AUTHOR:   Morgan, R.P.C.
             (Royston Philip Charles), 1942–
    TITLE:   Soil erosion and conservation / R.P.C. Morgan
ALT TITLE:   Soil erosion & conservation
  EDITION:   2nd ed.
PUBLISHER:   Harlow, Essex, England : New York, NY :
             Longman Scientific & Technical ;
             J. Wiley, 1995.
DESCRIPTION: 198 p.
 SUBJECTS:   Soil erosion.
CALL NUMBER: 631.45 MOR
```

Be sure to follow your school's Acceptable Internet Use Guidelines. They are designed to keep you safe when you use the Internet.

There are two common ways of finding information on the Internet:

1. If you know the exact Internet address (URL) you are looking for, type the address into the browser. (The browser is the computer software that lets you use the Internet.)

2. If you don't know the exact Internet address, you can use a search engine to find information. A search engine checks the whole Internet for Web sites that contain your word or phrase. This is called a **keyword search**. Here are some suggested sites:

   → Yahooligans (**www.yahooligans.com**)

   → Google (**www.google.com**)

   → Ask Jeeves for Kids (**www.ajkids.com**)

If you can't find what you want with one search engine, try another.

How to Do a Keyword Search

- Choose your keywords carefully. Use words that describe the topic you are researching.

- If you use a phrase, put it in quotation marks: "erosion of topsoil".

- You may get a long list of sites to view. The ones that match your keywords the best will be at the top.

- Don't be surprised if many of the sites do not seem helpful. It often takes a while to find good information.

- If you get too many sites or the wrong kind of information, add keywords to narrow the search.

Information on the Internet can be accurate and up-to-date, but it can also be misleading or wrong. Check to see who created each Web site you use. Ask yourself whether information from that source can be trusted. If you are not sure, ask an adult.

Here are more suggestions about using the Internet:

→ You can bookmark useful sites so you can return to them easily another time.

→ Some sites have links to other sites about the same topic.

→ The World Wide Web changes every day. Record your information while you are visiting the site. Don't wait until later.

Recording Information

You record information by making notes. There is no one way to make notes. But your notes should be well organized. The more organized they are, the easier it will be to prepare the final report. Here are some suggestions for recording information:

→ Read each source carefully.
→ Locate the main ideas.
→ Write the information in your own words.
→ Do not write down everything you find! Record only the information that relates to your topic and subtopics.
→ You can add to or revise your notes as you find new information or get new ideas.

There are different ways of recording information.

1. Point-form Notes

Point-form notes do not use complete sentences. They express ideas in the fewest possible words.

- erosion a big problem
    - loss of topsoil
    - danger of mudslides and rockslides
    - pollution carried into rivers and lakes

2. Graphic Organizer

A graphic organizer shows ideas in a visual way. It can help you see connections more clearly. There are many kinds of graphic organizers, such as the timeline and the KWL chart.

Timeline

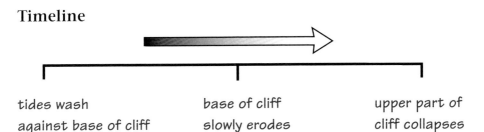

| tides wash against base of cliff | base of cliff slowly erodes | upper part of cliff collapses |

K-W-L Chart

K-W-L stands for What I Know, What I Want to Know, What I Have Learned. A K-W-L chart can help guide your research.

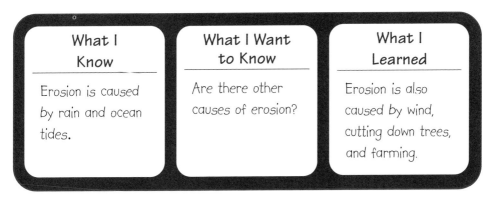

What I Know	What I Want to Know	What I Learned
Erosion is caused by rain and ocean tides.	Are there other causes of erosion?	Erosion is also caused by wind, cutting down trees, and farming.

See other graphic organizers on pages 129-140.

3. Index Card

Use one index card to record one fact or idea. Later you can group the cards with related ideas.

> Erosion occurs because of natural causes and because of human activities.

Organizing Information

Successful research often results in a lot of information. You don't have to use all of it—in fact, that would probably be a bad idea. How do you choose the information you should use? Here are some ideas:

1. Use index cards or cut your notes into sections. Sort them.

2. Choose the ideas that seem most important to you. Notice how the information was presented in the original source. Did it have its own page or chapter? Were there visuals with it? If so, they are probably worth keeping.

3. Choose information from the most up-to-date sources.

4. Don't repeat any information.

Make an outline. An outline shows the main ideas and their order. Some writers create an outline before they research while others do it afterward.

How to Create an Outline

- Use point form.
- Use each main heading as a new subtopic.
- List items that explain each subtopic.
- Do not repeat ideas.

Here is an outline that has been started.

A. Causes of Erosion
 1. Natural
  a. rainfall
  b. tides
  c. freezing

 2. Human Activities
  a. logging
  b. agriculture
  c. construction

B. Possible Solutions

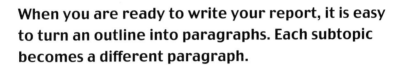

When you are ready to write your report, it is easy to turn an outline into paragraphs. Each subtopic becomes a different paragraph.

For another outline, see page 12.

Research

Giving Credit

Any time you use someone else's words or ideas you must say where they came from. As you research, keep a record of each source you use—each book, CD-ROM, encyclopedia, or Web site. You need this information so you can give credit to the original author.

There are two ways of giving credit.

1. Quotations

Most of the time you will write the information you find in your own words. But sometimes you will want to use the author's exact words. If you do, be sure to record the author's words carefully. Put quotation marks around them.

> There are several things we can do to stop erosion. Anton Juric, from *Save Our Soil*, says, "Planting grasses is a good way of protecting topsoil from wind and water."

Strategy

How to Avoid Plagiarism

Borrowing words and ideas without giving credit is called plagiarism. This is viewed as cheating. Here are ways to make sure you don't plagiarize work by accident:

- Do not cut and paste material directly from the Internet into your own work.
- When you make notes, always record the source of your information, including the page number.
- Always write your notes in your own words.
- Include quotation marks in your notes when you copy an author's exact words.

2. Bibliography

A bibliography is a list of the sources you used to find information about your topic. It appears at the end of a project or report.

List the resources in alphabetical order by the author's last name. Follow the punctuation you see in the examples below.

Record books like this:

Martino, Raheef. *Our Planet Earth*. Toronto: Heatstone
   Publishing, 2002.

Record CD-ROMs like this:

The Canadian Encyclopedia. World Ed. CD-ROM. Toronto:
   McClelland & Stewart, 2001.

Record Web sites like this:

"Action Plan to Improve Student Learning," Nova Scotia
   Department of Education, March 22, 2002. Internet
   www.ednet.ns.ca

Managing Your Time

Do you ever feel that there isn't enough time to finish your work? Learning to manage your time well can help. For bigger projects, follow these suggestions.

1. Be sure you know

   → what the main task is
   → when the work must be completed
   → how long the work will actually take
   → what resources you will need to complete the task

2. Break the main task down into smaller pieces, and then schedule each one.

Sample Outline

Today's Date: April 2

Task: Earth Science Project   Due on April 26

Do research   April 10

Make outline   April 12

Write first draft   April 19

Revise   April 23

Edit and Proofread   April 24

Final project   April 25

How to Use a Planner

A planner is a combination of a book and a calendar. It shows all the days of the year in order and gives you space to write what you need to do each day. Here are some tips for using a planner:

- List the things you need to do and when each is due. Include things such as studying for tests, daily homework, chores, and special events.

- Number each item in order of importance.

- Try to complete the items in that order.

- Check off each item as it is completed.

- If you don't get something done, move it to the next day in the planner.

November 20__

11 Monday
~~Test - social studies~~

12 Tuesday
Assignment due - math ✔

13 Wednesday
Field Trip

November 20__

14 Thursday
①. Assignment due - science
②. Band practice
③. Study for test.

15 Friday
Test - social studies

16 Saturday/17 Sunday

Part 4

How Writers Improve Their Style

Contents

Improving Your Style

What happens when you improve your writing style? Your writing becomes easier to understand and more interesting to read. Writing style is shaped by paragraph structure, sentence variety, word choice, and other factors.

WRITING STYLE

Paragraphs

Sentences

Words

Paragraph Structure

A paragraph is a group of sentences about one main idea or topic. A paragraph might describe an event, present an argument, or give facts about something.

What would books look like if there were no paragraphs? Every piece of writing would be a solid block of print. Paragraphs tell the reader when the writer is changing from one idea to another.

The rules about paragraphs are simple:

→ Indent the first line of every paragraph.

→ Start a new paragraph every time you move to a new idea.

→ With dialogue, start a new paragraph when the speaker changes. See Quotation Marks, page 120.

Paragraphs often contain three kinds of sentences.

1. The topic sentence states what the paragraph is about. It is usually the first sentence in the paragraph, but can be placed later.

2. Supporting sentences tell more about the main idea. They add details, examples, definitions, facts, and reasons.

3. The closing sentence sums up the main idea or makes a comment about it.

    Pioneers had to face many hardships. It was difficult to clear land for farming. Building houses and barns was a lot of work. The winters were harsh, and often there were food shortages by spring. Through determination, the pioneers were able to overcome these difficulties.

Sentence Variety

Sentence variety is the mixing of different kinds of sentences in writing.

If your sentences are always the same, the reader will lose interest. Sentence variety is the answer. You can create sentence variety by changing

→ the length of your sentences
→ the type of sentence you use (see Sentence Types, page 111)
→ your sentence structure (see Sentence Structure, page 110)

The paragraphs below show how sentence variety can add to a piece of writing.

Simple Sentences

Ali put on his roller blades. He set up his street hockey net. His friend Kyle joined him. Kyle played goalie. Ali took his first shot. Kyle robbed him. Kyle made one save after another. Ali gave a big shout when he finally scored.

Sentence Variety

Ali put on his roller blades and set up his street hockey net. His friend Kyle, a goalie, joined him. Kyle robbed Ali on his first shot, and kept making one save after another. When he finally scored, Ali gave a big shout.

Style

Transition Words

> Transition words link the sentences within a paragraph. They can also be used to link paragraphs.

Using transition words well can improve your writing. They help the reader move smoothly from one idea to the next. Here are a few common transition words and phrases.

according to	for example	now	though
after	fortunately	perhaps	unfortunately
although	however	since	unless
another	lastly	sometimes	until
because	maybe	soon	when
finally	meanwhile	still	whether
first	next	then	while

In the following example, the transition words are in bold.

What is the first true sign of spring? **Perhaps** the first sign is the sound of birds singing again after a long winter. For some people, **however**, the first sign of spring is water in the basement. **Unfortunately**, we had a big flood in our basement last week.

Formal and Informal Language

Informal language is casual, like the language you use when you talk to friends.

Formal language is more polished and polite, like the language you use when making a presentation.

The chart below shows the main differences between formal language and informal language.

Formal Language	Informal Language
• uses proper grammar	• may break grammatical rules
• avoids using contractions	• may use contractions
• avoids using slang	• may use slang
• focusses on the information, not the writer	• may include the writer's feelings

Formal language isn't better than informal language. Each kind of language is right for certain kinds of writing. The chart on the next page provides some ideas.

Style

Use formal language for ...	Use informal language for ...
• a report or presentation	• an e-mail to a friend
• a letter to someone you don't know	• a diary entry
• a newspaper article	• dialogue in a story or script

Here are two examples that show the difference between informal and formal language.

Informal

We had an awesome time at the circus. Everything was perfect. Sweet seats. And my aunt gave me ten bucks to spend. I liked it when the ringmaster announced all the acts. The clowns made me laugh so hard. But the trapeze act was my favourite. I sure didn't want the show to end. And I can't wait to go again!

Formal

The circus is a place where both the young and the old can have an exciting time. There is so much to see. The ringmaster announces all the different acts. The clowns will make you laugh and the people on the trapeze will make you hold your breath. Once you have been there, you will probably want to go again!

Word Choice

Word choice is the art of picking specific words that make your writing powerful.

Some words are not effective. The words *nice*, *good*, *said*, and *went* are a few examples. The reader hardly even notices these words because they are used so often.

To improve your writing, look for dull adjectives and weak verbs. Replace them with words that are more detailed and vivid.

Before	Better
• He had a **nice** smile.	• He had a **welcoming** smile.
	• He had a **youthful** smile.
• "Hi," Jessica **said**.	• "Hi," Jessica **shouted**.
	• "Hi," Jessica **growled**.

Writer's Tip

Use a Thesaurus

A thesaurus is a book of synonyms. It can help you find interesting words to replace words that are dull. If you look up *nice* in a thesaurus, you will find synonyms such as *pleasant*, *charming*, and *kind*.

See Thesaurus, page 86.

Style

Figurative Language

Figurative language uses words to create a picture in the reader's mind. It can surprise and entertain the reader.

Using figurative language is a way of playing with words. Here are three kinds of figurative language.

Similes

Similes use the words *like* or *as* to compare two unlike things. They help the reader see things in a new way, or show how two very different things can be similar in some ways.

> The autumn **leaves** were **as bright as fire** in the afternoon sun.

> **Sarah** swam **like a seal**, darting through the water.

Metaphors

Metaphors are a special type of comparison. Two unlike things or ideas are compared without using *like* or *as*.

> A **blanket** of snow covered the fields after the storm.
> (The covering of snow is like a blanket.)

Personification

Personification is another kind of comparison. The writer describes an animal or object as if it had human characteristics.

> The stream **babbled** its secrets as it bounced over the stones.
> (The stream is like a person talking.)

Sound Effects

In writing, the term sound effects refers to the sounds that words make when they are spoken aloud.

By playing with the sounds words make, you can make your writing come alive for your readers. They will "hear" your words in their imagination. Here are two different ways you can play with sound.

Onomatopoeia

Onomatopoeia is the use of words that imitate sounds, like *plop*, *zoom*, *crunch*, or *buzz*.

The dog's paws **sloshed** through the water.

The chimes **tinkled** in the wind.

Alliteration

Alliteration is the repetition of one consonant sound. The writer uses the sound several times in words that are close together.

The **w**hispering **w**ind **w**afted through the open **w**indow.

Sometimes alliteration is made by two consonants together.

The **gr**een of **gr**owing **gr**ass upon the waking **gr**ound is spring.

Style

Part 5

How Writers Edit Their Work

Contents

Word Use and Spelling

Grammar

Punctuation and Mechanics

Word Use and Spelling
Using References

Dictionary

A dictionary is a book of words and their meanings. The words are listed in alphabetical order.

You can use a dictionary to find out what a word means, how to spell it, and how to pronounce it. Some dictionaries tell the history of each word and show how to use the word in a phrase or sentence.

Guide words tell the first and last entry on the page. In the example on page 85, the guide words are **goblin** and **govern**. All the words between them alphabetically will be found on this page.

Entry word shows the spelling of the word and breaks it into syllables.

Pronunciation shows the phonetic spelling of the word.

Part of speech shows the word's part of speech. If the word can be used as more than one part of speech, all are listed.

Special forms show the spellings of some plurals or verb tenses.

Grammar and usage tells how words are used in certain ways.

Definition gives all the meanings of the word. There may also be illustrations to help explain the meaning.

Example shows how the word is used.

[guide words]

[entry word]

gob·lin (gob′lən) *n* in stories, a mischievous, ugly creature.

god (god) *n* a being that is worshipped; a being that people believe is greater and more powerful than any human. **–god′like′,** *adj.*
god·dess *n* a female god.

[pronunciation]

gog·gles (gog′əlz) *pl.n* a pair of large, close-fitting spectacles for protecting the eyes: *She wore safety goggles while she was welding.*

[part of speech]

gold (gōld) **1** *n* a heavy, soft, yellow precious metal. **2** *n* a bright, beautiful, or precious thing or material: *Wheat is prairie gold. Oil is often called* **black gold. –gold′en,** *adj.*
❦ **gold·eye** *n* a freshwater fish found in rivers and lakes from Ontario to the Northwest Territories. **gold·fish** *n* a small golden-orange fish kept in garden pools or indoor aquariums.

golf (golf) *n* an outdoor game played by hitting a golfball with different clubs. **–golf′er,** *n.*

gon·do·la (gon′də lə) **1** *n* a long, narrow boat with a high peak at each end, used on the canals of Venice. The person operating it is a **gondolier** (gon′də lēr′). **2** *n* a sort of box that hangs under a hot air balloon. **3** ❦ *n* a broadcasting booth near the roof of a hockey arena.

[definition]

gong (gong) *n* a piece of metal shaped like a disk or saucer, which makes a loud noise when you hit it.

good (gůd) **1** *adj* doing what is right: *a good boy, good deeds.* **2** *adj* well done: *a good piece of work.* **3** *adj* suitable: *Fresh air is good for the body.* **4** *adj* enjoyable: *Have a good time.*

[example]

5 *adj* skilled: *a good skater, good at math.* **bet·ter, best. –good′ness,** *n.*

Grammar ✓ Check ····· good

Need a good way to remember how to use the words **good** and **well** correctly? Try this.

• The word **good** is an adjective, so it always has a noun to describe: *a good way.*

• The word **well** is an adverb, so it always has a verb to describe: *You write well.*

So, using **good** and **well** correctly is *a good way to write well!*

[grammar and usage]

---

good·bye or **good-bye** (gůd′bī′) *n* farewell; what people say when they leave.
good-for-noth·ing *adj* worthless; useless.
good-look·ing *adj* handsome; attractive.

goods *pl.n* things that can be owned, bought, or sold: *Mr. Taylor left all his goods to his children.*
good·y *n Informal.* something very good to eat: *There were lots of goodies at the party.*
as good as, almost: *The day is as good as over.*
for good, forever; finally; permanently: *They have left Canada for good.*

Canada geese—
about 85 cm long
including the tail

goose (gūs) *n* a domestic or wild water bird larger than a duck. A male goose is a **gander.** A young goose is a **gosling.** *pl* **geese.**

[special forms]

go·pher (gō′fər) *n* a small furry animal of the prairies that lives mostly underground.

gorge (gȯrj) **1** *n* a deep, narrow valley. **2** *v* eat too much at once: *They gorged themselves on pizza.* **gorged, gorg·ing.**
gor·geous *adj* very beautiful.

go·ril·la (gə ril′ə) *n* the largest and most powerful ape.

gor·y (gȯ′rē) *adj* bloody; full of bloodshed. **gor·i·er, gor·i·est.**

gos·sip (gos′ip) *n* or *v* talk about other people and their personal lives: *Gossip is often hurtful and untrue* (*n*). *They gossiped on the phone for hours* (*v*). **gos·siped, gos·sip·ing. –gos′sip·y,** *adj.*

gouge (gouj) **1** *n* a deep scratch: *There was a long gouge in the desktop.* **2** *v* charge an unfairly high price: *They gouged us $40 for a plate of spaghetti.* **gouged, goug·ing.**

gourd (gůrd *or* gȯrd) *n* the squashlike fruit of a vine. Its hard, dried shell is used as a container in some cultures.

gov·ern (guv′ərn) *v* rule; control; manage: *Govern your temper. The premier and his or her cabinet govern the province.* **–gov′ern·ment,** *n,* **–gov′er·nor,** *n.*
Governor General in Canada, the representative of the Queen or King.

Thesaurus

> A thesaurus is a book that lists words that have the same or almost the same meaning. It also lists words that mean the opposite.

Use a thesaurus when you want to replace a dull word with a more interesting word. It can help you avoid using the same words too often.

Here is a sample entry in a thesaurus.

good *adj.* ① satisfactory, adequate, admirable, fine ② favourable, agreeable ③ virtuous, moral, true ④ clever, skilful, expert ⑤ appropriate, correct, valid, proper, suited *ant.* bad

When you look up a word in a thesaurus, how do you know which synonym to choose? Here are some suggestions:

→ Look up words you don't know in a dictionary to learn what they mean.
→ Compare the meaning and feeling of each word.
→ Try out the different synonyms in the sentence you are writing.
→ Ask yourself which word sounds best and has the right feeling.

Prefix

A prefix is a word or syllable that is put at the start of a word to change its meaning. The spelling of the rest of the word usually stays the same.

Most prefixes have one meaning. When you see an unfamiliar word, look for a prefix. It can help you understand what the word means.

This chart shows common prefixes and their meanings.

Prefix	Meaning	Examples
anti-	against	antifreeze, antiwar
bi-	two	bicycle, bilingual
dis-	not	disadvantage, disagree
fore-	at or near the front, before	forehead, forearm
im- in- non- un-	not, the opposite	impossible incapable nonsense unable
mis-	wrong, bad	misbehave, misread
pre-	before	preview, prehistoric
re-	again	re-entry, refuel
sub-	under	submarine, subway
trans-	across	transport, transcontinental

Suffix

A suffix is a syllable or letters added to the end of a word to change its meaning or function. When the suffix is added, the spelling of the word often changes. Sometimes it also changes the part of speech.

Some suffixes have one meaning; others have more than one meaning. This chart shows common suffixes and their meanings.

Suffix	Meaning/Function	Examples
-able **-ible**	able	break**able**, depend**able** sens**ible**
-ed	in the past	skat**ed**, own**ed**
-ful	full of	hand**ful**, tear**ful**
-ist **-er** **-or**	what someone or something does	art**ist** work**er** act**or**
-less	without	pain**less**, end**less**
-ly	in a certain way	happi**ly**, soft**ly**
-ment	makes nouns from verbs	agree**ment**, pay**ment**
-ous	full of	joy**ous**, poison**ous**
-tion **-ation** **-ition**	makes nouns from verbs	construc**tion** explora**tion** addi**tion**
-ward	in a direction	home**ward**, west**ward**

Synonyms

Synonyms are words that mean the same thing or almost the same thing.

You can find synonyms by looking in a thesaurus.
See Thesaurus, page 86.

Some common synonyms are

small — little	big — large	fast — rapid
shut — close	old — elderly	rich — wealthy

Antonyms

Antonyms are words that mean the opposite of each other.

Most thesauruses contain antonyms as well as synonyms.
See Thesaurus, page 86.

Some common antonyms are

small — big	up — down	fast — slow
shut — open	old — young	rich — poor

Homograph

Homographs are words that are spelled the same way but have different meanings, and sometimes a different pronunciation.

Here are two common homographs:

Bow means the front part of a ship <u>and</u> a decorative knot.

Bat means a flying mammal <u>and</u> a wooden stick used in baseball.

Homophone

Homophones are words that sound the same but are spelled differently and have different meanings.

Here are some common homophones:

pear — pair	bow — bough	maid — made
meet — meat	knew — new	write — right

Commonly Confused Words

Did you know that many spelling errors really are not misspellings? Instead, the writer confuses one word with another one and makes the wrong choice. Here are some of the words that are most often confused.

accept means *agree to*
except means *not including*
>   I am happy to **accept** this award.
>   Everyone had boots **except** Will, who had shoes.

all ready means *completely ready*
already means *before this time*
>   Is everybody **all ready** to go?
>   I've **already** seen that movie.

among is used for more than two
between is used for two only
>   There was one rose growing **among** the daisies.
>   Brenda sat **between** Hugh and Antonio.

desert means *a dry place*
dessert means *something sweet eaten after a meal*
>   The hot wind swept across the **desert**.
>   Latoya liked ice cream for **dessert**.

fewer is for quantities that can be counted
less is for quantities that can't be counted
>   I have **fewer** video games than you do.
>   Silvio has **less** lemonade than Midori.

Word Use

Commonly Confused Words

good is an adjective meaning *all right*
well is an adjective meaning *in good health* or an adverb
meaning *in a favourable manner*
> Sasha felt **good** about her award.
> I haven't been feeling **well** today. She speaks French **well**.

it's means *it is*
its means *belongs to it*
> **It's** very hot out today.
> The puppy sat up on **its** hind legs.

hear means *listen to*
here means *in this place*
> I did not **hear** what Sean said.
> Please pass the rice over **here**.

knew means *had knowledge*
new means *recently made*
> She **knew** how to spell the words.
> We all enjoy getting **new** clothes.

peace means *calm*
piece means *part*
> There is a feeling of **peace** down at the river.
> Lien hammered a nail into the **piece** of wood.

sit means *rest with the weight off your feet*
set means *put some place*
> I am going to **sit** in that chair over there.
> She **set** the vase of flowers on the table.

Commonly Confused Words

then means *at that time*
than is used for comparisons
> Finish your homework, and **then** you can watch TV.
> It is harder to hop **than** run.

there means *in that place*
they're means *they are*
their means *belonging to them*
> Put the books over **there** on the table, please.
> **They're** going outside for recess.
> The students performed **their** play.

to means *in the direction of*
two means *one more than one*
too means *also*
> I went over **to** the teacher.
> People have **two** eyes and **two** ears.
> Are we having dessert, **too**?

weather means *conditions outside*
whether means *if*
> In March the **weather** can be either cold or mild.
> Can you tell **whether** the door is locked?

you're means *you are*
your means *belonging to you*
> **You're** the kindest person I know.
> Is that **your** new jacket?

Spelling/Word Study

Correct spelling is important, especially in reports, formal letters, and other finished pieces of writing.

There is more to spelling than memorizing one word at a time. We remember words by learning different patterns of letters. Words with related meanings are often spelled in a similar way, as you can see from the following examples:

number — **num**erical   **sign** — **sign**al

We also remember letter patterns through

shape: though — although

sound: **pen** — **pen**cil

Learning letter patterns can help you with whole groups of words. The more you write, the more familiar you will become with the different patterns.

Spelling Strategies

If you need to spell an unfamiliar word, you might

→ Guess the spelling and then check it later.
→ Picture the word in your mind.
→ Try writing the word several ways. Which looks right?
→ Spell any small part of the word that you know—the root word, prefix, suffix, or syllables.
→ Think about words that sound the same that you can spell.
→ Check your personal dictionary or the Word Wall in your classroom.
→ Check with someone else.
→ Look in a dictionary.

How do you become better at spelling?

→ Try to spell words you don't know.

→ Clap out the syllables when you are learning a new word (make sure you have a vowel in each syllable).

→ Refer frequently to your personal dictionary or the Word Wall.

→ Practise writing and spelling aloud words that give you difficulty.

→ Note "tricky" words and find your own way to remember them.

→ Identify words every week that you find hard to spell. Use the strategy below to learn them.

Strategy

How to Spell New Words Independently

1. Choose the words you need to learn. Copy them carefully into your personal spelling list.

2. Read the first word. Look at it and say it.

3. Spell the word to yourself. Touch each letter and say it to yourself.

4. Close your eyes. See the word in your mind. Say each of the letters again to yourself.

5. Cover the correct spelling and write the word.

6. Check the word you just wrote, letter for letter, against the original.

7. If you spelled it correctly, go on to the next word. If you misspelled it, repeat the steps above.

Colloquialisms and Slang

A colloquialism is a word or expression that is used in everyday speech.

Slang is very informal language made up of new and colourful words and phrases.

We use colloquialisms and slang in everyday speech, but it is best to avoid both slang and colloquialisms in formal writing.

Here are a few examples of colloquialisms and slang, with suggestions for a more formal way of saying the same thing.

Colloquialism	Joan was **all ears**.
Formal Language	Joan listened **carefully**.
Slang	Dave was **pumped** about the holiday.
Formal Language	Dave was **excited** about the holiday.
Slang	Yuki's joke **bombed**.
Formal Language	Yuki's joke **was not funny**.

Inclusive Language

> **Inclusive language is language that encourages fairness and equality.**

Sometimes a piece of writing is biassed. It suggests negative ideas about a certain group in society.

Effective writers use inclusive language to avoid bias. Here are some suggestions that can help you make sure your language is inclusive.

→ Do not mention a characteristic such as gender, age, or ethnic background when it has nothing to do with the topic.

→ Do not use words that express stereotypes based on gender, race, ethnicity, disability, age, or religion. A **stereotype** is a false idea about a particular group. "Teenagers are troublemakers" is an example of a stereotype.

Gender

Sexist language belittles people based on their gender.

→ Do not use the word *man* when you are referring to people in general.

We need a strong **person** to help us move those bricks.

→ When you talk about different jobs, use words that include both men and women.

firefighter, letter carrier, salesperson, actor, police officer

→ Do not use *his* to refer to both men and women.

- Use the plural.

  Good **comedians** make **their** audience laugh.

- Use *her or his, her or him,* or *she or he.*

  Each student reads **his or her** essay out loud.

Disabilities

→ Avoid using *disabled* as an adjective. Use terms that describe the condition, not the person.

Our class did research to learn how people with disabilities are portrayed on TV.

Race and Ethnicity

Racist language belittles people who belong to a certain group.

→ Use the same terms that people in a group use to identify themselves.

members of the Black community, African-Canadians, Canadians of African ancestry

First Nations, Iroquois, Mi'kmaq, Cree

Grammar

Parts of Speech

There are eight main parts of speech. Every word in a sentence can be described as one of these parts of speech. A word can function as one part of speech in one sentence, and a different part of speech in another sentence.

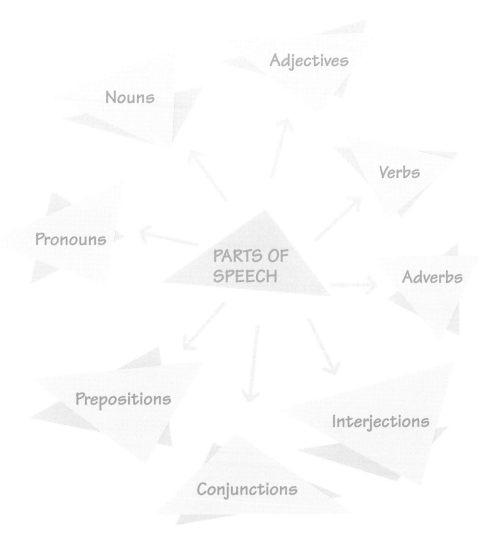

Noun

A noun is a word that names a person, place, thing, quality, or event.

Common nouns name general kinds of people, places, or things.

Proper nouns name particular people, places, things, or events. They always start with a capital letter.

	Common Nouns	Proper Nouns
Person	teacher	Ms. Johnson
Place	city	Halifax
Thing	school	Meadowland Elementary
Event	holiday	New Year's Day

Singular nouns (one) can become plural (more than one) in different ways. Most of the time, you just add the letter -s to the singular form of the word:

dog — dogs   road — roads   waterfall — waterfalls

The chart on the next page shows other ways to make plurals.

When a word ends with ...	You should ...	Example
s, ch, sh, or x	add -es	bus — bus**es** church — church**es** bush — bush**es** fox — fox**es**
y	change the y to i and add -es	baby — bab**ies**
	if a vowel comes before the y, just add -s	boy — boy**s**
f or v	change the f to v and add -es	hoof — hoo**ves**

Never use an apostrophe with an s ('s) to make a plural.

Exceptions

Some nouns are the same for both the singular and plural.

sheep   moose   fish

Some nouns become plural in unusual ways.

child — children   tooth — teeth   woman — women

mouse — mice   ox — oxen   antenna — antennae

goose — geese   die — dice   medium — media

Pronoun

A pronoun is a word that can be used in place of a noun to refer to a person, place, or thing.

Here are some different pronouns.

I	he	they
me	she	them
we	it	
you		

When you use a pronoun, you don't have to repeat the noun.

Janet and **Su** are going to the park. **They** will play on the swings there.

Does **Leo** know that **he** is going to be late?

The **cat** ran away because people make **it** nervous.

Verb

> **A verb is a word that expresses an action, event, or state of being.**

Natasha **rides** her bike to school. Yesterday she **fell** on her way home. Now she **has** a cut on her knee.

Verb Tense

The **tense** of a verb shows when an action or event takes place.

Past Tense	I **was playing** the piano yesterday.
	I **played** the piano yesterday.
Present Tense	I **play** the piano today.
	I **am playing** the piano today.
Future Tense	I **will play** the piano tomorrow.
	I **will be playing** the piano tomorrow.

Irregular Verbs

If a verb is regular, add -*ed* to form the past tense. An **irregular verb** does not use -*ed* to form the past tense.

Each irregular verb has its own special spelling to show the past tense. A dictionary will show whether a verb is regular or irregular. There are many irregular verbs. Here are a few:

Present	Past
begin	began
keep	kept
read	read
teach	taught
write	wrote

Writer's Tip

Use Vivid Verbs

Weak verbs such as *go*, *put*, *do*, and *walk* don't tell the reader very much. Strong verbs make your writing more precise.

Weak verb   Nicole **went** through the swamp.

Strong verb   Nicole **trudged** through the swamp.

Adjective

> **An adjective is a word that describes a noun or pronoun.**

Adjectives add meaning and help create pictures in the reader's imagination. An adjective is usually put just in front of the word it describes.

The attic was filled with **old** clothes and **broken** toys.

Adjectives can be used to make comparisons.

Comparative:

Add *-er* to show the idea *more*.   sweet — sweeter
                                                 neat — neater

Superlative:

Add *-est* to show the idea *most*.   sweet — sweetest
                                                 neat — neatest

With some words, you have to add *more* or *most*.

excited — more excited — most excited

Exceptions

Some adjectives change their spelling when you add *-er* or *-est*.

lazy — lazier — laziest   easy — easier — easiest

Some adjectives change their forms completely.

bad — worse — worst   many — more — most

Writer's Tip

Use Strong Adjectives

Some adjectives are weak. They don't give a reader enough information to form a clear picture in his or her mind. *Little, dark, big, old,* and *bad* are weak adjectives. Use specific adjectives that involve the five senses—sight, smell, taste, touch, and sound.

Weak   The **big** dog barked loudly.

Stronger   The **huge** dog barked loudly.

You can find strong adjectives in a dictionary or thesaurus.

Adverb

An adverb is a word that modifies a verb. It tells the reader more about the action—*how, when, where,* or *how often* it happened.

Adverbs often end in *-ly*: *quietly, gently, sweetly, carefully,* or *slowly.*

There are also other types of adverbs: *soon, here, very,* and *not.*

Julianna whispered **softly** to the scared puppy. When she **lovingly** scratched its head, the puppy looked up at her **adoringly**. Julianna knew that they would live together **happily**.

Preposition

A preposition is a word that shows the relationship of a noun or pronoun to another word in the sentence.

The following sentence shows how prepositions work:

The clown ran **around** the circus tent, **over** the bench, **up** the ladder, and **onto** the trapeze.

Here are some of the most common prepositions:

about	around	by	into	to
above	at	down	of	toward
across	behind	for	on	under
against	beside	from	over	upon
among	between	in	through	with

Conjunction

A conjunction is used to join words or groups of words.

Conjunctions join ideas together and show how they are related.

They decided to go outside **and** have a picnic. They had a good time **because** it was sunny.

Here are some common conjunctions:

although	but	since	unless
and	for	than	until
as	however	that	when
because	if	though	while

Some conjunctions are used in pairs: *either ... or; neither ... nor; not only ... but also.*

Angie is **either** first **or** second in line every morning.

Interjection

> **An interjection expresses an emotion, such as surprise, sadness, or happiness.**

Use an exclamation mark when an interjection expresses a very strong or sudden emotion.

Woohoo! We won the game.

Use a comma when an interjection expresses a mild emotion.

Aha, I found you at last.

Here are some common interjections:

ah	excellent	hurrah	oops	ugh
aha	great	oh	sh	well

Sentences

> **A sentence expresses a complete thought. Every complete sentence has a subject and verb.**

Sentences can be short or long. They can be simple or complex. But every complete sentence names someone or something (the **subject**) and tells what it does (the **verb**).

Both of the following sentences have just one subject and one verb. Notice, however, that they look very different.

subject verb
Donna sat.

subject   verb
The sleek brown otter, on a sunny afternoon, sat quietly on the warm rock.

Writer's Tip

Watch Your Subject/Verb Agreement

Both subjects and verbs can be singular or plural. In a sentence they have to match (agree with) each other.

subject verb
Singular   Gary likes pizza.

subject   verb
Plural   Dawson and Tess like pizza.

subject   verb
Singular   I am going to Ottawa.

subject verb
Plural   We are going to Ottawa.

Sentence Structure

Sentence structure refers to the order in which the parts of your sentence are put together.

Words in a sentence are like building blocks. They can be moved into different positions to change the way the sentence looks and sounds. These two sentences say the same thing, but in a different order:

Order #1   Sal loves to sing when his favourite music is playing.

Order #2   When his favourite music is playing, Sal loves to sing.

Some sentences have a simple structure, while others are complex.

Simple   Liz walked over the frozen pond.

Complex   Her skates, which she bought at a yard sale, were her favourite pair.

Strategy

How to Vary Your Sentence Structure

- Change the way you start your sentences. Don't start them all with *the* or someone's name.

- Use long, descriptive sentences to help the reader see the scene. Watch for run–on sentences. See Run–on Sentences, page 113.

- Use short sentences to create a fast pace or build suspense.

- Include questions that ask the reader to think about what you are writing. Don't forget the question marks.

Sentence Types

There are four sentence types: statements, commands, questions, and exclamations.

Type	Punctuation	Example
A **statement** gives information.	period	The doctor took the patient's temperature.
A **command** gives an order.	period	Take off your dirty boots.
A **question** asks something.	question mark	Do you have to go home?
An **exclamation** shows emotion.	exclamation mark	Oh, I just love that idea!

Phrase

A phrase is a group of words that has a meaning of its own even though it is not a complete sentence.

You can use phrases to add specific information to your sentences.

Basic Sentence	I got a drink.
Sentence + Phrase	I got a drink **out of the refrigerator**.

Common Grammatical Errors

Sentence Fragment

> The word "fragment" means *a part of something*.
> A sentence fragment is a group of words that does not express a complete thought.

A complete sentence contains a subject and a verb. A sentence without either a subject or a verb is a fragment. Although sentence fragments are common when you are speaking informally, they shouldn't be used when you write.

Fragment	Almost finished.
Complete	Scott has almost finished.
Fragment	The winners!
Complete	The Bobcats are the winners!

Run-on Sentence

> **Two or more sentences put together without proper punctuation create a run-on sentence.**

A run-on sentence has to be broken into smaller sentences that are correct.

Run-on   They searched for arrowheads but didn't find any instead they found some tin cans and plastic.

Correct   They searched for arrowheads but didn't find any. Instead they found some tin cans and plastic.

(made two sentences)

When fixing a run-on sentence using a conjunction, use a comma with *and, or, but, nor,* or *yet.*

Run-on   Travel books are good sources of information you can interview someone who has been to that country.

Correct   Travel books are good sources of information, or you can interview someone who has been to that country.

(used a comma and the conjunction *or*)

Double Negative

A double negative is the use of two negative words in a sentence.

You can fix a double negative by eliminating one of the negative words.

Double Negative   I **don't** have **no** money.
Correct   I **don't** have money. OR I have **no** money.

Pronoun Error

A common pronoun error involves the pronouns *I* and *me*. To fix the error, you replace *I* with *me*, or *me* with *I*.

Incorrect   Peter and me rode to the harbour.
Correct   Peter and I rode to the harbour.

Incorrect   She gave candies to my friends and I.
Correct   She gave candies to my friends and me.

Strategy

How to Check for Pronoun Errors

Try saying the pronoun by itself with the verb.
[Peter and] me rode to the harbour.

If the result sounds wrong, change the pronoun.
[Peter and] I rode to the harbour.

Indefinite Pronouns

> **An indefinite pronoun does not refer to a specific person or thing.**

When you use an indefinite pronoun, you must make sure the verb agrees with it.

anybody	each	everything	somebody
anyone	everybody	nobody	someone
anything	everyone	nothing	something

Singular indefinite pronouns need a singular verb.

Everybody is here now.

Plural indefinite pronouns need a plural verb.

both	few	many	several	others

Many are already at the party.

For some indefinite pronouns you can use either a singular or plural verb.

all	any	more	most	none	some

More are coming.   **More is** coming.

Agreement

In the past, we used the words *he*, *him*, and *his* to refer to people in general. Today we use words that include both males and females. See Inclusive Language, page 97.

Biassed	**Each** of the students handed in **his** work to the teacher.
Inclusive	**Each** of the students handed in **his or her** work to the teacher. (use both genders)
	OR
	All of the students handed in **their** work to the teacher. (change to plural)

We and *Us* Before a Noun

Sometimes you use the pronouns *we* and *us* before a noun. To see if you made the right choice, read the sentence without the noun.

Incorrect	**Us** [sports fans] like to go to as many games as possible.
Without the noun	**Us** like to go to as many games as possible.
Correct	**We** sports fans like to go to as many games as possible.

Punctuation and Mechanics

End Punctuation

End punctuation shows where a sentence ends.

Punctuation Mark	Type of Sentence (see p. 111)	Example
Period [.]	statement command	I went to see a movie. See a movie.
Question mark [?]	question	Did you go to see the movie?
Exclamation mark [!]	exclamation	It's a fantastic movie!

Apostrophe [']

1. **An apostrophe shows that one or more letters have been left out.** Sometimes two words are joined to make one word. One or more letters are left out, and an apostrophe is put in their place. The new word is called a **contraction**.

let us — let's	do not — don't
I am — I'm	you have — you've
I will — I'll	they are — they're
we would — we'd	cannot — can't

    Exception: will not — won't

2. **Apostrophes show ownership or possession.**

Tim's pita   the class's concert

the cat's food (one cat)   the cats' food (more than one cat)

3. **Apostrophes show that certain parts of a word are not spoken.**

the 'hood (neighbourhood)   'lectric (electric)

Comma [,]

A comma is used to separate elements in a sentence and to tell the reader to pause.

1. **Commas separate the words in a list or series.**

When there are three or more items in a list, put a comma between each one. Use the word *and* before the last item on the list.

She carried a math book, a notebook, a pen, and her lunch in her backpack.

2. **Commas separate the words in a date or address.**

On Tuesday, April 23, the class will go on a field trip to the zoo.

3. **Commas separate an introductory word or phrase from the rest of a sentence.**

No thanks, I think I'll stay here.

4. Commas set off the name of a person being addressed.

Jackie, would you like some more pie?

5. Commas set off words or phrases that interrupt a sentence.

Julian enjoys cooking with his older sister, Megan, on Saturdays.

Jenna plans to go skating with Cathy, her oldest friend, tomorrow.

Strategy

How to Fix a Comma Splice

A comma splice happens when two sentences are put together with a comma. A comma is not strong enough to hold two sentences together.

One solution is to divide the sentence into two.

Comma Splice	The crowd waited and waited for the concert to start, many of the kids became restless.
Correct	The crowd waited and waited for the concert to start. Many of the kids became restless.

Sometimes you can place a conjunction after the comma.

Correct	The crowd waited and waited for the concert to start, and many of the kids became restless.

Quotation Marks [" "]

> **Quotation marks show the actual words that someone speaks.**

This passage shows examples of quotation marks. The numbers refer to the points on the next page.

① Mr. Wilson looked proud. He pulled a piece of paper out of his coat pocket. "Look at this notice, Dr. Watson," he said. "You may read it for yourself."

I took the paper from him.

"What can it mean?" I asked.

② Holmes gave a chuckle then said, "It is a little odd. Isn't it? Do tell us more, Mr. Wilson."

③ "I own a store at Coburg Square," said Wilson. "It's a very small place. It has not done much more than give me a living. I used to have two helpers. Now I can pay only one. I can pay him only because he will work for half pay. I

④ don't know what I would do without him."

⑤ "Hmmm. A good helper who works for half pay," said Holmes. "And what is the name of this nice young man?"

⑥ "Vincent Spaulding," replied Wilson. "Oh, Vincent does have his problems. He is always down in the basement. He plays with all those cameras of his down there. A real photo nut. But on the whole he's a very good worker ..."

Using Quotation Marks

① Put the words a person says inside the quotation marks.

② If you start by telling who is speaking, use a comma before the quotation marks.

③ If you explain who is speaking after the quotation marks, use a comma, exclamation point, or question mark inside the quotation marks. Put a period at the end of the sentence.

④ Put the period at the end of a quotation inside the quotation marks.

⑤ Use lower case for the part that names the speaker unless it is at the start of the sentence.

⑥ Start a new paragraph every time a different person speaks.

Writer's Tip

Don't Use *Said* Too Often

The word *said* can get boring when it is used many times in a long section of dialogue. There are other words you can use instead. Words such as the following help you show the emotions of the people who are speaking.

grumbled	shouted	whispered	exclaimed
snorted	cried	chuckled	sighed

Colon [:]

A colon is used to introduce something. It tells the reader there is more information coming.

1. Colons introduce a list.

   Her gym bag was filled with gear: skates, a helmet, extra pucks, warm socks, and shin pads.

2. Colons separate the title and subtitle of a book.

   The Story of the Three Pigs: A Fractured Fable

3. Colons separate the hour and minutes when writing time.

   12:25 p.m.   6:00 a.m.

Writer's Tip

Use Punctuation You Understand

You may find that some punctuation marks are easier to use than others. For example, you may know how to use question marks but not colons. It's good to experiment with punctuation—that's how you learn. But when correctness is important, avoid punctuation you don't know well. If the punctuation "feels" wrong, rewrite the sentence using punctuation you understand.

Semicolon [;]

> **A semicolon is stronger than a comma, but not as strong as a period.**

Semicolons can connect two related sentences. They take the place of a conjunction.

The jogger ran through the park; it was the fastest way home.

Dash [— or --]

> **A dash is one long horizontal line or two hyphens. It shows a pause or break in a sentence.**

A dash indicates a break in a sentence such as a sudden change in action, thinking, or feeling. It is also used to show a pause in dialogue.

The detective froze in her tracks—then raced down the stairs.
(break in action)

I wondered what that strange sound was—until I opened the door!
(break in thinking)

"I tried to help her but—" said the firefighter.
(interruption in dialogue)

Hyphen [-]

> **A hyphen is one short horizontal line that connects numbers, words, or parts of words.**

A hyphen is more of a spelling mark than a punctuation mark. It shows connection.

When Hyphens Are Used	Example
in numbers from 21 to 99	twenty-five
in fractions that are written out	two-thirds
between syllables when a word is broken at the end of a line (Note: never split a proper noun or a one-syllable word.)	The dictionary uses dots to show where the syllable breaks are.
in some compound words that express one idea	son-in-law
in words that work together as an adjective in front of a noun	red-headed child ten-year-old car
in page numbers	pages 17–31
in game scores	6–5
in some words that start with prefixes	re-create co-operation

Ellipsis [...]

> **An ellipsis is three periods in a row that are used to show that words are missing from a sentence.**

An ellipsis indicates that someone has paused to think or did not complete his or her thoughts.

I'm thinking of cooking some chicken for supper, but then again ...

"You see, Sir ... well ... um ... the dog ate my homework."

Parentheses [( )]

> **Parentheses contain a word or phrase so it is set off from the rest of a sentence.**

Use parentheses to add information that you don't want to be part of the main sentence. They help the reader follow the idea smoothly.

The whole family (but not Dad) wanted to go skiing for the holidays.

That dog bites (which I know from personal experience).

Capitalization

Capital letters are also sometimes called upper case letters.

Use capital letters ...	Examples
to begin sentences or quotations	Lina was rushing. Graham mumbled, "Hold your horses."
for all proper nouns (see Proper Nouns, page 100)	Ricardo Diaz, Dr. Lee Fredericton, New Brunswick
for the main words in titles—the first word, the last word, and every word between that conveys meaning	Lord of the Rings The Simpsons Beauty and the Beast The First of Many Steps
for titles and family names	I asked Mom for a ride.
for days, months, and holidays	Sunday, January, Divali
for businesses and organizations, political parties, and religions	The United Nations, The Progressive Conservative Party, Islam
for historical events, eras, and documents	Confederation, The Information Age, The Constitution Act
for celestial bodies	Saturn
for all the letters in acronyms	BTW (by the way)
for special effects	BOO!

Abbreviations

An abbreviation is the shortened form of a word or phrase.

Use Abbreviations ...	Abbreviation	Example
for titles before a name	Mr. (Mister) Ms. (Mistress) Dr. (Doctor) Rev. (Reverend)	Mr. Mohammed Ms. Ramos Dr. Stevens Rev. Beaudoin
for *saint* in place names	St.	St. Lawrence River St. Croix Island
for time expressions	a.m. (or A.M.) p.m. (or P.M.) B.C. (Before Christ) B.C.E. (Before the Common Era)	3 a.m. 9:30 p.m. the year 67 B.C. 200 B.C.E.
for company or organization names	YWCA UNICEF	Women of all ages can enjoy programs at the YWCA that are designed especially for them. UNICEF is a worldwide charitable organization.
for addresses on envelopes	Rd Apt AB	320 Courtice Rd Apt 412 Red Deer AB

Other common abbreviations you may want to use in your writing include

e.g. — for example   i.e. — that is

etc. — and so on, and others   no. — number

Co. — Company   N.B. — note

Inc. — Incorporated   pp. — pages

Writer's Tip

Use Abbreviations Appropriately

Sometimes abbreviations are not acceptable. In formal or school writing it is best to spell out the entire word. Here are some other suggestions:

- Avoid using short forms as slang (information, not info).

- Don't abbreviate months (September, not Sept.), days (Monday, not Mon.), or places (Nova Scotia not NS).

- Avoid starting a sentence with a numeral (One hundred and fifty years ago ... not 150 years ago ...).

Graphic Organizers

Sometimes it's difficult to begin writing. You have so many thoughts in your head that you don't know where to start. A graphic organizer is a tool you can use to explore your ideas. It can also help you present ideas more clearly.

→ Use graphic organizers before you begin writing or researching to discover what you already know.

→ Use graphic organizers while you research to record and connect ideas.

→ Use graphic organizers when you write to help you present information.

Types of Graphic Organizers

Concept Web

A concept web allows you to explore what you already know about one main idea. You put the main idea in the middle of the web and put one related idea in each circle around the main idea.

The sample below shows a concept web in which BIRDS is the main idea.

Classification Chart

You can use a classification chart to organize facts or details about several related items or ideas. Each item is a heading in the chart, and the facts are listed underneath.

This classification chart organizes information about different kinds of transportation.

Bicycle	Car	Airplane
• quiet	• slightly noisy	• very noisy
• no pollution	• creates air pollution	• creates air pollution
• carries one person	• carries several passengers	• carries many passengers
• not good for moving heavy objects	• good for carrying heavy objects	• can carry freight
• good for short distances	• useful for long journeys	• good for travelling long distances
• inexpensive	• expensive	• needs a pilot • expensive
• requires human energy	• needs gas	• needs fuel

Venn Diagram

A Venn diagram is used to compare and contrast two people, things, events, or ideas. Each thing being compared has its own circle. Write the similarities in the space where the two circles overlap. The differences go in the other part of each circle.

Below is a Venn diagram that shows a few similarities and differences between whales and sharks.

WHALES
- warm-blooded
- skin
- produce milk
- get oxygen
  from air

- live in water
- eat fish (some)

SHARKS
- cold-blooded
- scales
- do not produce milk
- get oxygen
  from water

Flow Chart

A flow chart shows the order of a series of events. It can help you organize the events in a story or show the different steps of a process. For example, you could use a flow chart to describe the steps in an experiment.

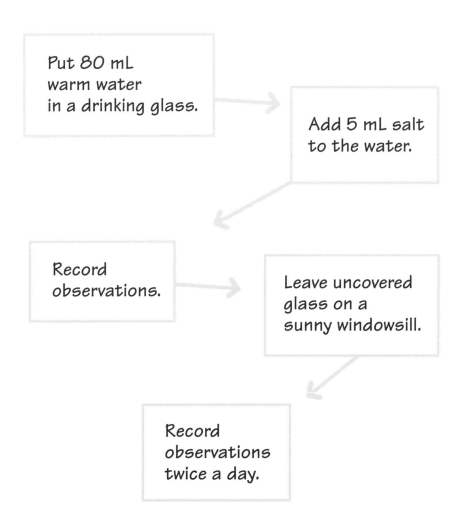

Put 80 mL warm water in a drinking glass.

Add 5 mL salt to the water.

Record observations.

Leave uncovered glass on a sunny windowsill.

Record observations twice a day.

Cause and Effect Chart

A cause and effect chart can help you understand an event. It asks you to think about why a particular event happened (the causes) and the results that followed (the effects).

In the chart below, the event is a flood.

CAUSE

heavy
snowfall

CAUSE

sudden
thaw

EVENT

FLOOD

EFFECT

damage to
houses

EFFECT

roads
washed out

Compare and Contrast Chart

A compare and contrast chart shows how two or more people, things, events, or ideas are similar and different. Across the top, write the name of each item you want to compare. Down the side, write specific qualities or features that are important.

The chart below compares diamonds and chalk.

	Diamonds	Chalk
colour	colourless	white
lustre	glittery	dull
streak	none	white
hardness	very hard	very soft

Cycle Diagram

A **cycle diagram** shows how one set of events happens again and again. The events in the process are placed in order and connected by arrows.

The cycle below shows the different stages of a frog's life.

Frogs lay their eggs in a pond or stream.

SPRING

FALL

Tadpoles hatch from the eggs.

Frogs return to the bottom of the pond or stream for the winter.

Tadpoles slowly develop into frogs.

SUMMER

Adult frogs breathe air instead of water.

Timeline

A **timeline** shows the order in which a number of events happened. (You can also use a timeline to show a plan of future events.) Many timelines include dates as well as a description of each event.

The following timeline shows a few important moments in Canadian sports.

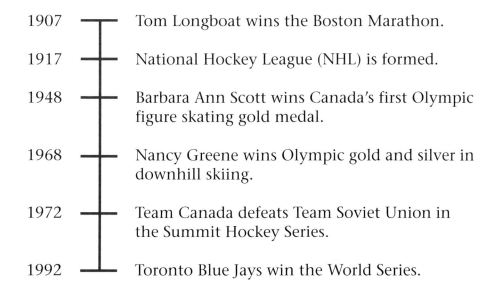

1907	Tom Longboat wins the Boston Marathon.
1917	National Hockey League (NHL) is formed.
1948	Barbara Ann Scott wins Canada's first Olympic figure skating gold medal.
1968	Nancy Greene wins Olympic gold and silver in downhill skiing.
1972	Team Canada defeats Team Soviet Union in the Summit Hockey Series.
1992	Toronto Blue Jays win the World Series.

For another example of a timeline, see page 65.

Tree Diagram

A **tree diagram** is a good way of showing connections between people, things, or ideas. For example, a family tree is a common kind of tree diagram. In a tree diagram, the main idea or ideas are at the top, and related ideas are placed underneath.

Below you can see how a tree diagram can help you classify objects or ideas.

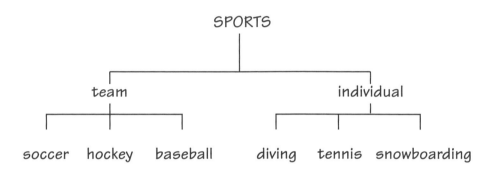

See the example on page 60 that shows how you can use a tree diagram to narrow a topic.

K-W-L Chart

A **KWL chart** is usually used during the research process. It can help you see what you already know about a topic and what additional information you should seek. KWL stands for What I Know, What I Want to Know, and What I Learned. You can see an example of a KWL chart on page 65.

You can add an extra column to a KWL chart to make it a KWHL chart. The H column stands for How I Can Find Out. It encourages you to think about the specific resources that might help you with your research. Below you will see a KWHL chart a student might use for researching the author Monica Hughes.

What I Know	What I Want to Know	How I Can Find Out	What I Learned
• Monica Hughes is a Canadian writer. • She writes science fiction for young readers. • One of her books is called *Crisis on Conshelf 10*.	• When was she born? • How did she become a writer? • How does she get ideas for books? • What books has she written?	• Use a search engine on the Internet. • Check the school library for her books. • Write her a letter.	• She was born in 1925 in Liverpool England. • She wrote lots of stories and books before she got published. • She jots down her ideas and keeps them in a file.

Story Map

A **story map** is an organizer that can help you plan a story. By completing a story map, you think about some important parts of your story before you start writing. (Of course, you can change your mind if you think of better ideas while you are drafting your story!)

Most story maps ask you to consider things such as setting, characters, conflict, and plot. You can see an example on page 33.

Other story maps, like the one below, are simpler.

Beginning
A ten-year-old boy is invited to fly across the country by himself and stay with his aunt and uncle for the summer. Although he is worried about being away from home, he says yes.

Middle
The boy's aunt and uncle help out at a shelter for the homeless. At first the boy doesn't know what to expect at the shelter. He soon makes many friends, and he learns that each person has an interesting story to tell about his or her life. The boy decides to make each of his friends a small but special gift.

End
When the boy is ready to return home, the people at the shelter organize a surprise party for him and give him a gift of their own.

Glossary

Abbreviation   An abbreviation is the shortened form of a word or phrase.

Adjective   An adjective is a word that describes a noun or pronoun.

Adverb   An adverb is a word that modifies a verb. It tells the reader more about the action.

Apostrophe [']   An apostrophe is a punctuation mark used to show ownership, letters that are missing, or parts of a word that are not spoken.

Audience   The audience is the people who will be reading your writing.

Alliteration   Alliteration is the repetition of one consonant sound.

Antonym   Antonyms are words that mean the opposite of each other.

Bibliography   A bibliography is a list of the sources you used to find information about a topic. It is placed at the end of a report.

Colloquialism   A colloquialism is a word or expression used in everyday speech.

Colon [:]   A colon is used to introduce something, such as a list. It tells the reader there is more information coming.

Comma [,]   Commas are used to separate elements in a sentence and tell the reader to pause.

Command   A command is a sentence that gives an order.

Conflict   Conflict is a problem that has to be solved by the character in a story.

Conjunction   A conjunction is used to join words or groups of words.

Dash [— or --]   A dash is one long horizontal line or two hyphens that show a pause or break in a sentence.

Dialogue   Dialogue is the words characters speak to each other. Quotation marks are used to show when dialogue starts and ends.

Drafting   Drafting is the stage when you start to express your ideas in writing.

Editing   Editing is the stage when you correct sentence structure, language, and grammar.

Ellipsis [...]   An ellipsis is three periods in a row that are used to show that words are missing from a sentence.

End Punctuation   End punctuation shows where a sentence stops.

Exclamation   An exclamation is a sentence that shows emotion.

Exclamation Mark [!]   An exclamation mark is a kind of end punctuation that shows a sentence is an exclamation.

5 Ws and H   The 5 Ws and H are the six questions every newspaper article should answer—*who, what, when, where, why* and *how*.

Graphic Organizer   A graphic organizer shows ideas in a visual way.

Homograph   Homographs are words that are spelled the same but have different meanings and sometimes a different pronunciation, for example, *bow* and *bow*.

Homophone   Homophones are words that sound the same but are spelled differently and have different meanings, for example, *pear* and *pair*.

Hyphen [-]   A hyphen is a short horizontal line that connects numbers, words, or parts of words.

Imagery   Imagery is the set of pictures "painted" in the reader's mind by a piece of writing. It is created by the descriptive words and phrases the writer chooses.

Inclusive Language   Inclusive language is language that encourages fairness and equality.

Interjection   An interjection expresses an emotion, such as surprise, sorrow, or delight.

Lead A lead is one or more opening sentences that grab the reader's attention. In a newspaper article, the lead usually answers the 5 Ws and H questions.

Metaphor A metaphor compares two unlike things or ideas without using *like* or *as*.

Noun A noun is a word that names a person, place, thing, quality, or event.

Onomatopoeia Onomatopoeia is the use of words that imitate sounds, for example, *buzz*, or *zoom*.

Outline An outline is a plan to show how your writing will be organized.

Paragraph A paragraph is a group of sentences about one main idea or topic.

Parentheses [()] Parentheses contain a word or phrase so it is set off from the rest of a sentence.

Period [.] A period is a kind of end punctuation that shows a sentence is a statement or command.

Personification Personification describes an animal or object as if it had human characteristics.

Point-form Notes Point-form notes express ideas in the fewest possible words. They do not use complete sentences.

Prefix A prefix is a word or syllable put at the start of a word to change its meaning.

Preposition A preposition is a word that shows the relationship of a noun or pronoun to another word in the sentence.

Pronoun A pronoun is a word that can be used in place of a noun to refer to a person, place, or thing.

Proofreading Proofreading involves the correction of spelling, punctuation, and capitalization errors.

Publishing Publishing involves making a good copy of your writing that is ready for other people to read.

Purpose The purpose is the goal of your writing.

Question A question is a sentence that asks something.

Question Mark [?] A question mark is a kind of end punctuation that shows a sentence is a question.

Quotation Marks [" "] Quotation marks are used to show the actual words someone speaks.

Revising Revising is the process of looking at your writing once again and making changes to improve it.

Rhyme Rhyme is the repetition of sound in different words, especially at the ends of words; for example, boy rhymes with toy.

Rhythm Rhythm is the arrangement of beats in a line of poetry.

Run-on Sentence A run-on sentence is formed when two sentences are put together without proper punctuation.

Semicolon [;] A semicolon is a punctuation mark that is stronger than a comma but not as strong as a period.

Sentence A sentence is a group of words that express a complete thought. Every sentence has a subject and a verb. There are four types of sentences—statement, command, question, and exclamation.

Sentence Fragment A sentence fragment is a group of words that does not express a complete thought.

Simile A simile uses the words *like* and *as* to compare two unlike things.

Slang Slang is very informal language made up of new and colourful words and phrases.

Statement A statement is a sentence that gives information.

Stereotype A stereotype is a false idea about a particular group. "Teenagers are troublemakers" is a stereotype.

Suffix A suffix is a syllable or letters added to the end of a word to change its meaning or function.

Synonym Synonyms are words that mean the same thing or almost the same thing.

Verb A verb is a word that expresses an action, event, or state of being.

Index